not a guide to
Leicester

Natasha Sheldon

The author wishes to express her gratitude to the
following people and organisations for the use of
their images: Neil Bate; Neil Hart; Groundwork
Leicester; Phil 'Steam' Shaw; Stephen McKay;
Peter Warzymski; Chris Worden; Kiran Parmar;
Andy T.; Occupy Leicester; Alun Salt;
Mat Fascione; Richard Rogerson; Ned Trifle;
the University of Leicester; and Pete Hackney.

First published 2013

The History Press
The Mill, Brimscombe Port
Stroud, Gloucestershire, GL5 2QG
www.thehistorypress.co.uk

© Natasha Sheldon, 2013

The right of Natasha Sheldon to be identified as the Author
of this work has been asserted in accordance with the
Copyrights, Designs and Patents Act 1988.

British Library Cataloguing in Publication Data.
A catalogue record for this book is available from the British Library.

ISBN 978 0 7524 9108 0

Typesetting and origination by The History Press
Printed in Great Britain

Coat of Arms

The wyvern is a fabulous beast that is part of the dragon family. It was a symbol of strength and valour for the old Kingdom of Mercia, of which Leicester was once part. The wyvern was also the insignia of Thomas, the city's second earl. Leicester's wyvern sits atop its coat of arms, flecked with blood. This commemorates Thomas's execution after his revolt against Edward II.

*

On the red shield is a cinquefoil – a symbol of hope and joy in the form of a white, five-petalled flower. This was the emblem of two of Leicester's Lancastrian earls: Robert De Bellomonte, and Robert Fitz Parnell.

*

The two red lions *rampant reguardant* wear the coronet of the Lancastrian duchy. They look backwards, perhaps into the past when Leicester was part of that duchy, before it was absorbed into the crown lands and ultimately became a free borough.

*

The motto *Semper Eadem* or 'always the same' was the personal motto of Elizabeth I. It was adopted by Leicester after the queen bestowed borough status upon the town at the end of the sixteenth century.

Contents

Leicester	6
The Shakespeare Connection	8
Grid Reference	10
Street Names	12
Districts and Wards	14
Distance From…	16
Local Bearings	18
Twin Towns	20
Other Leicesters	22
Historical Timeline	24
A Day in the Life of…	26
Demographics	28
Strange Statistics	30
Leicester in Days Gone By: Granby Street	32
Famous For…	34
Infamous For…	36
Letters to the Press	38
Buildings and Architecture	40
Leicester in Days Gone By: Gallowtree Gate	44
Museums	46
Parks and Green Spaces	50
Green Leicester	52
Favourite Food	54
Homegrown Businesses	56
Scientific Discoveries	58
Buried in Leicester	60
The Grave of Richard III	62
Heroes and Villains	64

Leicester in Days Gone By: The Corn Exchange	68
The Luddites	70
Rebellious Leicester	72
Crimes, Court Cases and Mysteries	74
The Witches of Leicester	76
The Legacy of Richard III	78
Leicester in Days Gone By: St Nicholas Church	80
Ghosts	82
Black Annis	84
Leicester Under Attack	86
Local Lingo	88
Festivals	90
Who Lived Here?	92
Authors	94
Musical Leicester	96
Leicester in Days Gone By: London Road	98
Political Figures	100
TV Personalities	102
Leicester Bollywood	104
Leicester and Royalty	106
Sporting Heroes	108
Leicester Tigers	110
Other Sports	112
Extreme Ironing	114
Particular Pubs	116
Leicester in Days Gone By: The Station	118
Not a lot of People Know That…	120
Future Plans	122
Before You Go…	124
Picture Credits	126

Leicester

Pronounced /lɛstər/ LESS-tər

Leicester's name retains elements of its Celtic, Roman and Saxon past – and a bit of legend too. According to Geoffrey of Monmouth, the city was the 'Fort of Leir', the British king of Shakespearean fame who legend says made the town his bastion.

The only fort that history acknowledges was built by the Romans, who founded Leicester in around AD 50. Then it was known as *Ratae Corieltaurorum* – 'the walled place of the Coritani', the local Celtic tribe whose capital it became.

The city's modern name combines the memory of its *castra* or fort with the name of the River Soar which runs through it. To the local Celts, the river was *Legra*, which translated into Saxon as *Leir*. By AD 803, Leicester was recorded as *Legorensis Civitatis* or 'the settlement of the people of Leir'. By the tenth century, the name had evolved again into *Legra Caester* – 'the town of the Legra people' before settling into its modern form.

The Shakespeare Connection

Geoffrey of Monmouth's legend of Leicester's foundation must have persisted, for in the sixteenth century a travelling player performing at the town's Guildhall supposedly heard it. When the actor took up the quill himself, he reputedly used the legend as the foundation for a play of his own. That travelling player was none other than Shakespeare, and the play *King Lear*.

The idea of Shakespeare's connection to Leicester was attractive enough for the city to erect a pub named the Shakespeare's Head near Southgates. In 2003, it also encouraged the Royal Shakespeare Company to follow in the bard's footsteps and perform at the Guildhall, as part of the BBC's *In Search of Shakespeare* series.

However, this new legend of Leicester, like that of Leir's foundation of the city, is nebulous at best.

Grid Reference

Clock Tower: SK 58761 04626

(143 metres from the geographical centre of Leicester)

Street Names

Street names are one of the few relics of Leicester's time under the Danelaw. The 'gate' in names such as **Belgrave Gate**, **Gallowtree Gate** and **Church Gate** does not relate to a portal but derives from *gata*, the Old Norse word for road.

Other streets preserve the former uses of the land they cross or pass. **Butts Close Lane** runs alongside the site of the town's former archery practice field. **Friar's Lane** and **Blackfriars** preserve the memory of the Franciscan and Dominican orders who once owned vast tracts of the land in the town.

Street names have also changed with time. The elegant-sounding **Newarke Street** was once known as Hangman's Lane because it led to the gallows outside the town. **Silver Street**, named after its former trade, was also known as Sheep's Market, Lychyrs Lane and Hot Street.

Some names changed after public petition. **Claremont Street** in Belgrave was known as 'Backside' before one of its residents objected. During the First World War, a public outcry led to German-sounding streets such as Hanover Street and Saxe-Coburg Street being amended to **Andover** and **Saxby Street**.

Other names record modern triumphs, with **Tiger's Way** honouring the town's successful rugby club.

Here's a selection of other interesting Leicester street names:

Holy Bones

Raw Dykes Road

Pingle Street

Frog Island

Cank Street

Pocklington's Walk

Districts and Wards

Modern Leicester is a hybrid, made up of the old town, former villages and rural land swallowed up over the years by the expanding city.

The Old Town
Abbey, Castle and Westcotes.

Local facts: Castle Ward extended in 1804 to absorb land south of the city walls. Nearby Westcotes was the crossing point for Roman Fosse Way and Watling Street. The area has provided many of Leicester's Roman remains.

Landmarks: Leicester Castle, abbey, city centre, Victoria Park, Leicester and De Montfort Universities and residential areas: Claredon Park with the Queen's Road shops and Westcotes's former factories, now apartments and bars.

Former Villages
Beaumont Lees, Belgrave, Humberstone and Hamilton, Evington, Braunstone, Aylestone, Knighton.

Local facts: Belgrave is either named after the grave of Bel, a local giant, or comes from the French for 'lovely grove'.

Landmarks: Historic buildings such as Belgrave and Aylestone Halls. The cores of old villages survive in places like Knighton, Evington and Braunstone. Belgrave is also home to the 'Golden Mile'.

Rural Land
Western Park, Stoneygate, Highfields, Eyres Monsell, Spinney Hills, Freedmen, Latimer, Rushey Mead, Charnwood, Thurncourt, New Parks, Fosse, Coleman.

Local facts: Stoneygate gained its name from the first Victorian villa built in the fields south of Leicester. Other opulent residences and a village followed. Windmills used to stand in the place of modern Highfield's Victorian terraces.

Landmarks: Western Park includes the Dane Hills, home of Black Annis. Stoneygate and Highfields have some of Leicester's finest examples of Victorian architecture.

Distance From...

Place	Miles	Km
Ayers Rock, Australia	9,336	15,025
Brussels, Belgium	266	427
Centre of the Earth	3,964	6,378
Death Valley, Utah	4,806	7,734
Eiffel Tower, Paris	301	485
Frankfurt, Germany	457	736
Glasgow, Scotland	255	410
Hong Kong, China	5,988	9,637
Istanbul, Turkey	1,620	2,607
Jerusalem, Israel	2,316	3,728
The Kremlin, Russia	1,562	2,513
Lima, Peru	6,297	10,134
The Moon	237,194	381,701
Niagara Falls, Canada	3,502	5,636
Osaka, Japan	5,840	9,398
Panama Canal, Panama	5,239	8,432
Queenstown, New Zealand	11,733	18,883
Reykjavik, Iceland	1,089	1,753
Syracuse, Sicily	1,338	2,153
The Taj Mahal, India	4,315	6,945
Ural Mountains, Russia	2,316	3,727
The Vatican, Rome	975	1,570
Washington DC, USA	3,822	6,150
Xanthi, Greece	1,450	2,334
Yellowstone National Park, USA	4,529	7,290
Zurich, Switzerland	564	907

Local Bearings

From the Clock Tower (Grid Reference SK58762 04626):

	Grid Reference	Distance
National Space Centre	SK 58795 06569	1,990m
University of Leicester	SK 59283 03001	1,710m
Abbey Park	SK58894 05835	825m
Leicester Castle	SK58216 04190	693.95m
Leicester Cathedral	SK58481 04455	326.35m
Walker's Stadium	SK58086 02950	1,810m
Tiger's Stadium	SK58789 03305	1,330m
Leicester Market	SK58768 04472	155m

19

Twin Towns

Strasburg, France
In 1960 Strasburg became Leicester's first twin as part of
the post-war movement to establish closer links between
Britain and Europe. The two cities also have space research
in common. Strasburg is the home of the European Audio-
Visual Observatory and the International Space University.
Leicester has the National Space Centre and Leicester
University's space research programme.

Krefeld, Germany
Like Leicester, Krefeld began as a Roman city. Both also
share a history in textiles. Leicester was once renowned
for its hosiery business while Krefeld specialised in the
weaving of silk and velvet. Twinned in 1969, the two cities
regularly arrange for exchanges of students and visits
between their sports clubs.

Rajkot, India
Many of Leicester's residents have connections with the
state of Gujarat, of which Rajkot is a major city, making
this twinning in 1986 a natural development. Leicester and
Rajkot also share a commitment to environmentalism.

Masaya, Nicaragua
Established in 1987, this twinning also celebrates diversity
and was instigated by the Leicester Masaya Link group.

Chongging, China
This twinning, established in 1993, was motivated by
economic growth.

Haskovo, Bulgaria
Leicester's newest twin established in 2008 aims to continue
to encourage the exchange of people across cultures.

Other Leicesters

	Miles	Km
Leicester, North Carolina, USA	3,990	6,422
Leicester, Massachusetts, USA	3,255	5,238
Leicester, New York, USA	3,470	5,584
Leicester, Vermont, USA	3,234	5,205

Historical Timeline

Leicester becomes part of the Danelaw.

Publication of Leicester's first weekly newspaper, *the Leicester Journal*.

Romans establish Ratae Coritanorum on the banks of the River Soar.

Norman Conquest.

William Wyggeston, Leicester's greatest benefactor is born.

Leicester loses its city status.

English Civil War: siege of Leicester by Royalist forces.

AD 50   877   1066   11thC   1467   1645   1753
      410   918   1068   1298   1485   1680s

Last Roman soldiers leave Britain.

Leicester's motte and bailey castle built by Hugh de Grantmesnil, the first Norman lord of Leicester.

Richard III stays in the Blue Boar Inn before the Battle of Bosworth Field.

24

Leicester recaptured for the Saxons by Aethelfleda, daughter of King Alfred.

Charter granted to hold a Saturday market in Leicester.

Beginning of hosiery trade in Leicester.

The last public execution in Leicester, that of William 'Peppermint Billy' Brown.

First air raid of the Second World War on Leicester.

Sir Peter Soulsby became the first directly elected mayor of Leicester.

The Swannington to Leicester railway opens.

St Martin's Church becomes Leicester Cathedral.

Asian refugees from Idi Amin's Uganda flock to Leicester.

1832   1856   1927   1940   1970s   2011

1785   1841   1919   1937   1957   1992

Britain's first pedestrianised walkway, New Walk, is built in Leicester.

King George V restores Leicester's city status in gratitude for its efforts in the First World War.

University of Leicester established in the buildings of the former county lunatic asylum.

The first Thomas Cook tour leaves Leicester.

The League of Nations declares Leicester to have the highest living standards of any city in the British Empire.

Leicester Polytechnic becomes De Montfort University.

A Day in the Life of Leicester

04:03   First train of the day leaves Leicester for London.

07:00   Early morning swimmers take to the pool at Aylestone Leisure Centre.

07:40   Morning prayers are said at the cathedral.

09:30   Ticket office opens for bookings at Curve Theatre in Leicester's cultural quarter.

10:00   The National Space Centre opens to visitors.

12:00   Shoppers take a break at the Highcross shopping centre to have lunch in one of the many bars and bistros surrounding its central piazza.

16:10   Last *Discovering Leicester* tour bus leaves the railway station.

18:30   Gold and sari shops begin to close along Belgrave Road, Leicester's Golden Mile.

19:00   Ghost walks start at Leicester Town Hall.

20:00   Diners tuck into a post-theatre dinner at Chutney Ivy, mentioned in the Michelin Red Guide.

22:45   Isha prayers begin at Leicester central mosque.

00:00   Closing time at the Polar Bear, one of the oldest pubs in Leicester.

Demographics

(Based on the 2001 census)

Total number of people: **279,921**

Males: **134,782**

Females: **145,139**

Ethnicity:
White: **178,739**

Largest minority ethnic group:
Indian or British Indian **72,033**

Religion:
Christian: **125,187 (44.72%)**

No religion: **48,789 (17.43%)**

Hindu: **41,248 (14.74%)**

Muslim: **30,885 (11.03%)**

Religion not stated: **19,782 (7.07%)**

Sikh: **11,798 (4.21%)**

Buddhist: **638 (0.23%)**

Jewish: **417 (0.15%)**

Other: **1,179 (0.42%)**

Employed: 52.98%

Unemployed: 4.88%

Number of students: 12.67%

Average age of the population: 37.6

29

Strange Statistics

3 shillings   Price paid in 1645 to Francis Motley for mending the doors of St Martin's Church after they were broken by Royalist forces.

10 a.m.   The time the first ever train left Leicester on 17 July 1832.

2,000   Number of people living in Leicester in 1086, according to the Domesday Book.

60,200   Number of people who passed through Leicester's east gates between 8 a.m. and 10 p.m. on 23 November 1861.

23st 3lb   Weight of the 'laughing policeman', PC John 'Tubby' Stephens, who died in 1908.

70   Number of unemployed Leicester men who marched to Manchester in search of work in 1909.

250   Number of rockets stationed on Victoria Park during the Second World War.

6,500   Number of electric lights used to illuminate Leicester's Golden Mile during Diwali, 2010.

100   Number of oaks used to build the roof of Leicester Castle's Great Hall in 1522.

11 million   Number of bags of crisps produced each day by Leicester's Walker's Crisp factory.

9ft 4in   Waist measurement of Leicester gaoler Daniel Lambert, who died in 1809.

6 days   Length of time Buffalo Bill's Wild West show stayed in Leicester in 1891.

700   Number of men needed to clear up heavy snowfall in the city in 1887.

£120,000   Average Leicester house price in 2009.

254,000   Number of hours taken to carve and assemble the Jain temple.

Leicester in Days Gone By:
Granby Street

Famous For...

Richard III
In September 2012, the last Plantagenet king's remains were recovered from a Leicester car park.

Leicester Market
Voted 'Britain's favourite market' in 2011, Leicester Market has sold goods on the same spot for over 700 years. It is the largest market of its kind in Europe.

Multiculturalism
From its beginning, Leicester has been a nexus point for diverse groups of people. Romans, Angles, Saxons, Danes and Celts all settled and traded in the city. Later, the prosperous hosiery and manufacturing business attracted people from across the globe. Today, Leicester is the most culturally diverse city in the UK. Indian, Pakistani, Eastern European, Somali and Afro-Caribbean populations – to name but a few – live alongside the descendants of those earliest incomers.

Birthplace of the Package Tour
The world's first package tour, organised by Baptist lay preacher Thomas Cook, left Leicester on 5 July 1841. For just one shilling each, Cook organised rail travel and food for 570 temperance activists travelling from Leicester to Loughborough. By 1850, Cook had offices along Gallowtree Gate and was organising trips all over the world.

Largest Diwali festival outside of India
The Hindu festival of lights, Leicester's Diwali festival is the biggest outside India with the centre of festivities along Leicester's 'Golden Mile'.

National Space Centre
Opened in 2001, the centre is one of the UK's leading attractions, offering the chance for visitors to experience a range of exhibits and events related to space science and astronomy.

Infamous For...

Leicester's Lost Architecture

Post-war Britain was notorious for its careless clearance of the past. Leicester was no exception and many architectural gems were bulldozed to make way for modern buildings.

Amongst Leicester's lost architecture is the **Theatre Royal,** which stood on Horsefair Street until 1958. Not long afterwards, the **Temperance Hall** on Granby Street was demolished. This venue for two of Charles Dickens' legendary readings in Leicester was replaced by an ugly office block.

The Temperance Hall was not the only building connected to Dickens to be lost. **The Bell Hotel**, a coaching inn built in 1700, used by the author during his visits to the city, was torn down with many other period buildings in 1970 to make way for the Haymarket Shopping Centre.

Many locals feel that this modernisation of the city centre has in fact left it looking rather tacky and ripped out its heart.

'To Let' Signs

Many of Leicester's former banks, offices and shops now stand empty as the new Highcross development has shifted business away from the old city centre. With 104 out of 708 business units empty, Leicester is above the national average of 11%.

The worst hit areas are Church Gate, Gallowtree Gate and Humberstone Gate, with nearly one building in four vacant.

Letters to the Press

Towards the end of the First World War, *The Leicester Mercury* was bombarded with letters from irate readers demanding the removal of German-sounding street names. 'You can now help us to wipe out those names which remind us of memories we are trying very hard to forget,' stated one letter from a wounded solider.

Not everyone believed the paper could help. The Revd Cecil Robinson of St George's Vicarage, Saxe-Coburg Street, had a radical solution for a man of god. Although careful to state that he did not 'wish to incite violence', he believed 'the Irish method of bringing English authorities to reason is the only one that would be at all productive.'

Others saw the name debacle as a fuss over nothing. 'Why stop at street names?' suggested R. Arnold. 'There are some forty-odd German-named members of our body, such as finger, hand, arm etc. which should be at once renamed… In fact, a complete revision of our vocabulary is required to prevent all further use of German words.'

Less controversial but still unusual was an appeal in the same paper in the 1990s. A local Wigston man asked for information about a ghost reputedly haunting the former site of Parker's Meat Wholesalers on Freeman's Common. He received several replies telling tales of unexplained banging, misty forms and the mysterious movement of livestock for slaughter about the building.

Buildings and Architecture

Oldest Civic Building

Dating from 1390, the Guildhall was originally the meeting place for the Guild of Corpus Christi. It has subsequently been Leicester's Town Hall, library, police headquarters and court. Narrowly escaping demolition in the twentieth century, it survives as a museum and civic venue.

Biggest Eyesore

St George's Tower dominates the Leicester vista. The tower of the former British Telecom and Royal Mail building was never a pretty sight. It was made worse when redevelopers sprayed the structure bright blue with coloured squares, making it one of the city's most talked about landmarks – for all the wrong reasons.

Most Under-Budgeted New Building

Leicester's Curve theatre was only supposed to cost the tax payers £4.4 million. By the time the building opened in 2008, that figure had rocketed to £35 million. In total, the award-winning structure which dominates Leicester's cultural quarter cost £61 million.

Most Unusual Monument

After his retirement from Leicester police, Francis 'Tanky' Smith made a fortune as Leicester's first private detective. He invested his money in Top Hat Terrace on London Road. The houses, now a solicitor's office, are adorned with sixteen carved heads, commemorating Tanky in his famous disguises.

Most Confusing Building

With its crenelated turrets, Welford Road prison is often mistaken by tourists for Leicester's castle.

Most Unique Place of Worship

Built in 1980, Leicester's Jain temple is unique in the western world. The original Victorian chapel is covered with a façade of white marble, carved to imitate Jain architecture.

Leicester in Days Gone By:
Gallowtree Gate

Museums

Abbey Pumping Station. A former Victorian sewage works, Leicester's Museum of Science and Technology is situated next to the National Space Centre.

Key Exhibits: Four of the sewage work's beam steam engines. Three have been restored to full working order.

Belgrave Hall. Once the centrepiece of Belgrave Village, the hall preserves elements of Belgrave's rural past in its grounds and outbuildings. Inside, it offers a snapshot of the lifestyle of upper middle-class Victorian families.

Key Exhibits: Two acres of walled gardens and a stable yard where crafts are exhibited.

Jewry Wall Museum. Leicester's Museum of Archaeology is the next-door neighbour of the ruined Roman baths. Exhibits range from the prehistoric to the medieval period.

Key Exhibits: The Peacock Pavement, an exceptional mosaic floor salvaged from one of Leicester's Roman villas.

The Guildhall. The medieval guildhall and former Town Hall of Leicester.

Key Exhibits: The Victorian police cells, Great Hall and Richard III exhibition.

New Walk Museum & Art Gallery. Leicester's first museum offers a range of family orientated displays of historical artefacts and works of art.

Key Exhibits: Dinosaurs, Egyptian mummies and Picasso ceramics.

Newarke House Museum. Museum of twentieth-century Leicester and the Royal Leicestershire Regiment, the museum is composed of Wygston Chantry House and Skeffington House.

Key Exhibits: A series of rooms recreating different eras from the twentieth century; Daniel Lambert's clothes.

Parks and Green Spaces

Overall, Leicester consists of approximately 1,250 hectares of parks and open spaces. Some, like **Bede Park** along the city's waterside, are built on reclaimed industrial land. But most are the remains of estates, villages, fields and common ground.

Many Leicester parks still preserve historic features. **Abbey Park** consists of the grounds of the old abbey and meadows surrounding the River Soar. **Victoria Park**, which surrounds the University of Leicester, is all that remains of the south fields of the city. It was once home to the city's racecourse. Other parks and open spaces, such as **Knighton Park**, **Leicester Riverside's Aylestone Meadows** and **Watermead Country Park,** have areas of outstanding natural beauty or environmental significance.

Besides being used for walking, relaxing and playing, Leicester parks are used as venues for many of the city's festivals and events – **Castle Gardens** being just one example.

Other parks include:
Aylestone Hall Gardens; Beaumont Park;
Braunstone Park; Castle Hill Country Park;
Evington Park; Leicester University Botanical Gardens;
Monks Rest Gardens; Nelson Mandela Park;
Prebend Gardens; Rushmead Playing Fields;
Shady Lane Arboretum; Spinney Hill
Park; The Rally; Western Park

Green Leicester

Leicester has a proud green heritage. It was Britain's first environmental city in 1990 and its first European Sustainable City in 1996. In 2010, it came second in the Sustainable Cities Index, excelling in biodiversity, recycling of household waste and its ecological footprint. Its green innovations include:

The Ecohouse. Located in Western Park, this is the first environmental show home in the UK. Run by Groundwork Leicester, the house and its garden practically demonstrate how to live sustainably.

The Orange Bag Recycling Scheme. By increasing the types of recyclable waste it collects from city households, Leicester has doubled its recycling of rubbish to over 3,000 tonnes a week.

Park Force. An initiative which involves local people in planting and maintaining the city's parks.

Cycling. Initiatives to persuade residents to get 'on their bike' include hosting Sky Ride events across the community and the Leicester Cycle Challenge, where workplaces compete to see who can persuade the largest number of employees to cycle to work. Groundwork Leicester also run the Bikes4all scheme which recycles and rehomes bikes destined for landfill sites.

Leicester Fit4business. As an extension of the cycling scheme, Fit4business seeks to reduce carbon emissions and encourage economic growth. Central to the scheme are improvements to public transport in Leicester by creating more efficient bus links around the city.

Bioblitz. An annual event where city residents are encouraged to record as many species as possible in their local parks and open spaces during a set period of time.

Favourite Food

In 1759, Leicester's first cheese market was established to regulate local cheeses such as **Stilton** before they were exported across the country. Such was the town's reputation for quality that one variety, known as 'the Leicestershire cheese', was renamed **Red Leicester** in its honour. Leicester people today particularly enjoy this cheese sliced or grated over their chips.

Nearby Melton Mowbray may be the birthplace of the pork pie, but Leicester has its very own variety – the **Walker's pork pie**, developed by the same family of local butchers responsible for the famous crisps. Leicester residents have their own unique way of eating it too. Often served with brown sauce, a pork pie in Leicester can find itself in lunchtime sandwiches and as a replacement for the usual bowl of breakfast cereal – especially on Christmas Day.

These days, **samosas** replace the sausage roll at many a Leicester 'do'. Leicester won the title 'Curry Capital of Britain' in 2007 and the lower half of London Road heading into the city centre is lined with curry restaurants catering for the locals' love of all things spicy. But Belgrave is the place for a real **Leicester curry** with restaurants such as vegetarian Bobby's and former pub The Flamingo providing the authentic taste.

Finally, there is McIndians, who, with their cheeky name and motto, 'you've tried the cowboys, now try the Indians', have spiced up take away favourites such as fish and chips, and burgers.

Homegrown Businesses

Food is big business in Leicester – literally. **Walker's Crisps** were founded by local butchers, the Walker family, during the Second World War to compensate for meat rationing. The new sideline took off and today Walker's Crisps, now owned by PepsiCo, hold 47% of the British market with the snacks still produced in Leicester.

Fox's Glacier Mints were founded in 1918 by a local grocer. The small ice cube-shaped mints quickly became a national favourite with the introduction of Peppy the Polar Bear in 1922.

A favourite of chip shops country wide, **Pukka Pies** also originate in the city. Formed in 1963 by Trevor Storer, the company still produces 560 million pies a year in its Leicester factory.

Leicester's newest food enterprises belong to the city's Asian residents, capitalising on the British love of curry. **Leicester Bakery Ltd** is one of the largest manufacturers of speciality bread in the UK, distributing pittas and naan bread across Europe. Founded in 1990, family-run **Mayur Foods** is also now one of the UK's leading ethnic food manufacturers, producing traditional naans and chapattis as well as spices, sauces and pastes which are exported to over twenty countries.

Other businesses originating in Leicester and still going strong include:

Everards Brewery – Founded in 1849 and still brewing its cask ales in Leicester.

Dunelms Mill – A nationwide textile and home furnishing chain.

Gadsby's – Fine art and picture-framing business founded in 1890.

Scientific Discoveries

Two of Leicester's biggest scientific discoveries occurred as by-products of other research. During the 1970s, Professor Ken Pound's research into X-ray astronomy at Leicester University led to the discovery of **black holes**, revolutionising space research. Today, Leicester University is one of the largest academic space research centres in Europe and Professor Pounds is regarded as a leading expert in the field. Despite being courted by both NASA and the European Space Research Organisation, he continues to maintain Leicester as his base.

In 1985, Leicester University scientist Alex Jefferies was working on the genetic coding of muscles. He noticed that each chromosome had a completely individual 'bar code' of genetic information, meaning that every individual had their own unique pattern of DNA. **DNA fingerprinting** has subsequently revolutionised forensic science, helping identify criminals and resolve paternity issues. It has also earned Professor Jefferies a knighthood.

In recent years, the university has made a vital breakthrough in the **treatment of malaria**. Leicester researchers have discovered new ways in which the parasite which causes the disease can survive in the blood, helping in the development of improved anti-malarial drugs.

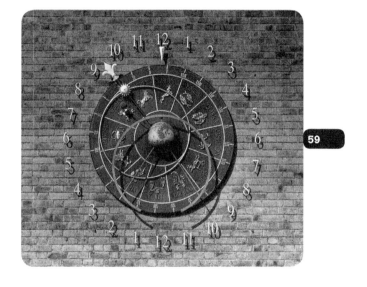

Buried in Leicester

Leicester's Welford Road Cemetery is the last home of many a famous Leicester resident. **Thomas Cook** and **Mary Linwood**, the celebrated embroideress given the freedom of Paris by the Emperor Napoleon, are both buried there. But Leicester is also the last resting place for many non-residents who died just passing through the town, often in less than tranquil circumstances.

In November 1530, **Cardinal Wolsey**, Henry VIII's former chancellor, found himself at Leicester Abbey. The cardinal was on his way back to London but the journey was not a happy one. The disgraced prelate had been called to answer a charge of high treason. Fortunately for him, perhaps, his journey ended in Leicester. He died at the abbey on 29 November and was buried there. A stone commemorates him today.

The Grave of Richard III

After the Battle of Bosworth Field, **Richard III**'s naked corpse was brought to Leicester. For two days it was on display in the church of St Mary of the Annunciation, where De Montfort University's Hawthorn Building now stands. It was then claimed by the friars of the Franciscan order and quietly interred in the local Greyfriar's church.

Ten years later, Henry VII contributed £60 towards providing the man he had defeated with an alabaster tomb. But with the Dissolution of the Monasteries in 1538, the exact site of Greyfriars and its church was lost. As for Richard, a local legend grew that the defeated king suffered one last indignity when his corpse was disinterred and thrown without ceremony into the River Soar.

On the 500th anniversary of the king's burial, University of Leicester Archaeological Service began an excavation to rediscover the site of the lost Greyfriar's church. One of their first finds under what was the church's choir was a man's skeleton. The body, whose spine was deformed, was buried naked, without a shroud or coffin. His hastily dug grave was too small to accommodate his full length.

After five months of tests, and a comparison of the DNA of the remains with those of King Richard's descendents, the university declared that it had indeed found the remains of the last Plantagenet king.

Leicester will remain the site of Richard III's grave when the king is reinterred with honour at Leicester Cathedral, just over the road from his original grave.

Heroes and Villains

John Merrick, the Elephant Man

Self-educated and courteous, Merrick's courage in the face of adversity makes him a true Leicester hero. Born in Lee Street in August 1862, Merrick was rejected by his family after the death of his mother. He spent four years in Leicester workhouse before leaving Leicester at twenty-one with Sam Torr, a travelling showman he persuaded to hire him.

Daniel Lambert

At 5ft 11in tall, Leicester gaoler Daniel Lambert was well-built and fit, until his mid-twenties. Despite eating moderately, only drinking water and being so keen on swimming he taught the local children, by the time he was thirty-five he weighed 52 stone 11lb. He lived until he was thirty-nine, dying after visiting Stamford Races. Leicester's fattest man, he is remembered affectionately for his optimistic approach to life.

William Wyggeston

Born in 1467, Wyggeston was a wealthy wool merchant who was twice lord mayor of Leicester. He was also the town's richest man. Leicester's biggest benefactor, he founded the Wyggeston Hospital and the town's first grammar school.

Simon De Montford

The 6th Earl of Leicester is credited with introducing the first elected Parliament to England in 1265. De Montford's stand against the tyranny of the Crown made him a hero. But he was also something of a villain, expelling the Jews from Leicester in 1255. Jews were forced to earn a living through usury. De Monfort's persecution of them was a cunning way of winning popularity with the people of Leicester by freeing them from their creditors.

Leicester in Days Gone By:
The Corn Exchange

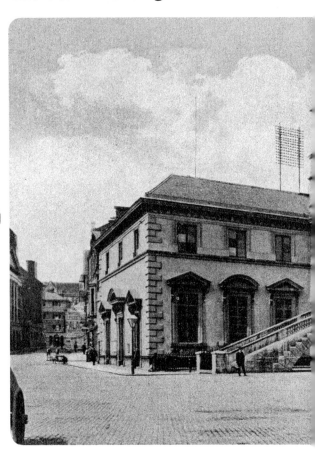

The Luddites

One man's hero is another's villain. In the early nineteenth century, the Luddites were regarded as a threat to the social order by the establishment. But to the textile workers of Leicester they were heroes and martyrs.

Ned Lud was a simple-minded man from Anstey, just outside Leicester. One day, he escaped the taunting of local boys by hiding in a cottage, where he broke the owner's knitting frame in a rage. From then on, if anything was broken, local people claimed 'Ned Lud' was responsible.

Thirty years later, the textile industry had moved from cottages to factories. But the outlook was not good for weavers and stocking knitters. Employers began to look for ways to manufacture cheaply. Mechanisation was the key and many Leicestershire hosiery workers faced the loss of their livelihood.

Then, factory owners began to receive letters threatening their machines. The letters were signed 'Ned Lud'. Mysterious men began to break into factories and destroy the equipment. They became known as Luddites after the signature on the letter.

Machine breaking, however, had been made a capital offence by a ruling class terrified that social unrest would lead to revolution. In 1816, after smashing eighty-five machines in a Loughborough factory, James Towle and Ben Badder were sent to the gallows in Leicester. They died without naming any of their accomplices. Unfortunately, the next year a member of the gang was caught poaching. To save his own neck, he sent Towle's brother, William, and five others to swing in his stead.

Rebellious Leicester

The Luddites aren't Leicester's only industrial rebels. In 1787, workers rioted after Coltman and Whetstone tried to introduce steam-powered stocking-making machines in their factories. This was followed in 1886 by several thousand striking hosiery workers breaking factory windows. And, as recently as November 2011, thousands of public sector workers marched through Leicester city centre in protest against pay and pension cuts.

But it's not just industrial disputes that have the people of Leicester up in arms.

Bowstring Bridge, 2009
Built in 1890, Bowstring Bridge was one of only three railway bridges of its kind in the world and unique in the UK. But after it became unsafe, the structure was threatened with destruction. Despite a spirited protest by Leicester Civic Society and a 6,000-strong petition, the bridge was demolished in 2010.

Anti-capitalist protests, 2011
During Christmas 2011, Leicester's High Street became a camp for around forty anti-capitalist protestors. 'Occupy Leicester' consisted of students and many locals who joined the camp after work. The protest spread to a deserted pub, the Littern Tree, before the camp was served with eviction notices and many of the protestors left because of chest infections.

Aylestone Meadows, 2011
One of the city's most controversial planning applications was defeated by environmental activists in 2011. The proposal, which would have seen a floodlit football pitch built on part of Aylestone Meadows Nature Reserve, was defeated by local people who marched in protest and set up the first E-petition on Leicester City's Council's website.

Crimes, Court Cases and Mysteries

In 1832, twenty-one-year-old bookbinder **John Cook** went on the run after burning the remains of John Paas, a London engineer he owed money to, in the fireplace of his workshop. The quantity of smoke alerted neighbours who called officials to investigate. The officers were suspicious of the charred remains, which Cook claimed to be gone-off dog food, but rather than arrest him on the spot, they told him to make himself available for further questioning. Instead, Cook hot-footed it for Liverpool that very night. He was apprehended just as he was about to board a boat for America. He was tried and hanged in Leicester. Ironically, the seal on his indictment was made by his victim.

The Green Bicycle Murder is one of Leicester's most enduring mysteries. In 1919, twenty-one-year-old Bella Wright was murdered as she cycled home from her uncle's house. Before her death, she was seen talking to a mysterious man on a green bicycle. Bella was later found shot through the head on Gartree Road. In 1920 Ronald Light, a teacher from Highfields, was arrested after his own green bicycle was found in the Grand Union Canal. Light claimed to have disposed of the bicycle when he became afraid of the media frenzy following the murder. He was sensationally acquitted. Many people believed he did indeed kill Bella. But it has also been suggested that she may have been accidentally shot by boys taking pot shots at crows.

The Witches of Leicester

In 1616, in a trial reminiscent of Salem, nine women were executed for bewitching thirteen-year-old John Smyth. The boy claimed he was possessed by the witches' animal familiars, who supposedly induced their victim to make a variety of bestial noises. Some years later, James I visited Leicester. Obsessed by witchcraft, the king questioned John. He confessed that he had lied to the court.

The last indictment for witchcraft in a UK secular court took place in Leicester in 1717. Jane Clare of Wigston Magna, with her son and daughter, were publicly swum before being taken before a Leicester court. Twenty-five witnesses stood against them but the enlightened jury threw the case out.

Today, witches are the winners in Leicester. In 2007, the *Telegraph* reported that a local coven had prevented Leicester's new shopping complex from being named 'The Highcross Quarter'. The developers claimed they simply wanted to commemorate the town's old high cross, which was once located in the area. But to the witches, it was a misuse of a term used for the festivals of the Wiccan calendar.

The witches used the power of the internet rather than magic to stake their claim by registering a number of domain names. Strangely, despite offering to buy the rights and, when that failed, threatening to taking the matter to the United Nations' World Intellectual Property Organisation, the developers suddenly dropped their claim and opted for the name 'Highcross' instead.

The Legacy of Richard III

Witches also play their part in the story of Richard III. Before the Battle of Bosworth Field, Richard stayed in Leicester. As he departed the town, the king reputedly hit his spur on a stone of the Bow Bridge. A local witch prophesised that Richard would return the same way – but on the return journey it would be his head, not his heel, that struck the bridge.

Richard's ghost supposedly haunts Grey Friars. But what he left behind him in the Blue Boar Inn is said to have led to the creation of another of Leicester's ghosts.

The king brought his own bed to Leicester and left it at the White Boar Inn. After his defeat, the inn, named for Richard's own emblem, wisely changed its name to the Blue Boar Inn. But the bed reputedly remained. So did a secret hidden within it.

In 1613, the landlord, Thomas Clarke, found a cache of gold coins worth £300 in a false bottom beneath the bed. The find made Thomas and his wife Agnes wealthy but they still continued to run the inn. But Thomas's death left Agnes vulnerable. A plot was hatched by one of the inn's maids and a local man to rob the landlady. Agnes put up a fight but she was overpowered and choked to death. Her ghost was said to haunt her former domain until it was demolished in 1836. It then transferred to the new Blue Boar Inn on Southgate Street, before that too was demolished in the 1960s.

Leicester in Days Gone By:
St Nicholas Church

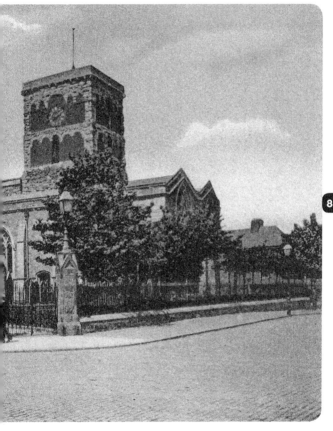

Ghosts

As befits one of Britain's oldest cities, Leicester has a whole array of ghostly residents.

The Guildhall is the most haunted building in the city, with at least five resident spirits including a ghost dog and a Victorian police constable. The most famous is the 'white lady' who appears at night, rearranging the furniture of the library. When displeased, the ghost is said to unlock doors and set off alarms. She also has a fondness for the museum's ancient bible which, although closed at the end of each day, is always found open at the same page.

Another white lady has been seen inside **Leicester Cathedral** on several occasions. Outside, the cathedral has a more sinister spirit. One of the churchyard trees is haunted by a misty crouching figure. Local legend advises not to go near if this spook is spotted – for if it touches you, you will be dead within the year!

This unpleasant ghost isn't the only misty manifestation in Leicester. The **Longstop Pub** along Churchgate is apparently haunted by a former landlord, Harry Staines, who fell down its cellar steps in 1896. Other haunted pubs include the **Marquis of Wellington** on London Road and the **Talbert Inn** in Belgrave, reputedly the most haunted pub in Leicester. Both were stopping points for felons on their way to the local gallows.

Other haunted buildings include:
Braunstone Hall

Belgrave Hall

Blackfriars Hall

Wygston House

The Haymarket Theatre

Goldsmith Music Library

Friar Mills

Black Annis

The ghosts of executed felons have also been seen in the Great Hall of Leicester Castle. But its southern entrance has a far stranger manifestation. This is supposedly haunted by a ghoulish figure once used to frighten local children into obedience: Cat Anna or Black Annis.

Annis's origins are complex. She may have begun life as a benign Celtic fertility goddess named Anu or Danu, who gave her name to her original home, the Dane Hills. With the rise of Christianity, Anu's benign elements were overlooked in favour of some of the less savoury elements of Celtic goddesses, particularly the death hag aspect. Sacrifices to the goddess, which may have survived in the form of the Easter Monday Drag Hunt, where a dead cat soaked in aniseed was dragged from the Dane Hills to Leicester, led to the goddess becoming a demon. Gentle Anu became grisly Annis, a blue-faced monster with long teeth and talons who would drag off stray children to her cave and devour them, hanging their skins from a nearby tree.

The Dane Hills are now part of a housing estate just off Glenfield Road. Legend tells that they are connected to Leicester Castle by an underground passage. Perhaps Annis isn't so keen on having neighbours, which explains why she has abandoned her former home for the relative quiet of Leicester Castle.

Leicester Under Attack

Siege of Leicester

On 31 May 1645, pro-Parliamentary Leicester was besieged by Royalist troops led by Prince Rupert. The aim of the attack was to draw Cromwell's New Model Army away from Oxford and the king. The town garrison of 2,070 men continued to fight against the Royalist forces even after the city walls were breached. In revenge, Prince Rupert allowed his men to loot the town of 140 cartloads of gold and silver including the corporation mace and insignia.

Leicester's Blitz

Unlike many cities in the UK, Leicester got off lightly as far as bombing attacks were concerned. But the night of 19 November 1942 can be viewed as the night of Leicester's blitz. For over eight hours, 150 bombs and parachute mines were dropped over an area of the city stretching from the Aylestone gasworks to Belgrave Road.

IRA

The first bomb to go off in Leicester in 1939 was Irish, not German. On 9 June 1939, an IRA parcel bomb exploded at the Campbell Street sorting office next to the railway station. The attack was intended to increase pressure on a British Government already preoccupied with imminent war. No one was killed but the building was gutted by the explosion.

A second attack occurred just over fifty years later in 1990, when a Semtex bomb was hidden under a car outside the army recruitment office. By coincidence, this is not far from Campbell Street.

Local Lingo

Much of the everyday language of traditional Leicester folk is derived from Norse or Anglo-Saxon words and greetings. Here's a quick guide to some of the words and phrases you might encounter in Leicester.

Greetings
Ey up – hello

Me duck – sir/madam

Mi chip – brother

Ey up our kid/me old fruit – friendly greeting

Old cock – friend

Worro – hello

Food and drink
Chip ole – chip shop

Gollop – eat/drink fast

Larrup – pop/beer

Snaps – lunch

Exclamations
Ah oraah – yes

Ay up – way of attracting attention, to give a warning

Ooh yer bug – you don't say!

Ooooyawh beggaw – goodness me!

Ooo ya bewteh – amazing

Emotions
Lairy – mad

Chuffed – pleased

Chin on – grumpy

Cobbon – upset

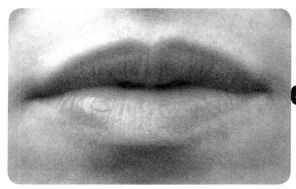

Festivals

It's probably no exaggeration to say that Leicester has a festival for every month of the year. Besides Leicester's famed **Diwali** celebrations, which lead seamlessly into the **Christmas** festivities, there are a diverse range of other community celebrations.

In August there is the **Caribbean Carnival,** with its spectacular procession through the streets of the city, culminating at Victoria Park. Leicester also holds celebrations for **Chinese New Year**, **Holi**, **Dashera and Hanukkah**. It is also the only major UK city to significantly mark the Hindu festival of **Navratri**.

The city also commemorates its long history with annual events such as the **Castle Park Festival** and the **Riverside Festival.** There are also plenty of annual arts and entertainment events. **Dave's Comedy Festival**, the longest running of its kind in Europe, which has featured comedians such as Sarah Millican and Russell Howard, is celebrated annually, as is the **Belgrave Mela** – a celebration of South Asian music and dance.

Other Leicester festivals include:

St George's Festival

Bonfire Night on Abbey Park

The St Patrick's Day Parade

The Spark Children's Arts Festival

The Big Session Festival

Summer Sundae Weekender

Leicester International Music Festival

Leicester Pride

Who Lived Here?

Thorncroft House, London Road. Home of **Thomas Cook**. The house was marred by tragedy when Cook's daughter, Annie Elizabeth, died here in mysterious circumstances after she was forbidden to marry her lover.

College House, Leicester University. Childhood home of **Sir David** and **Lord Richard Attenborough**. The family moved to Leicester in 1932 when their father became Principal of the then University College, Leicester. Richard began to act in the city's Little Theatre. David began to develop his passion for the natural world though regular visits to Leicester Museum on New Walk.

118 New Walk. Now part of the Belmont Hotel, this was the former home of **Ernest Gimson**, 'the greatest of the English architect-designers' and one of the leading members of the Arts and Craft movement. Gimson also designed many of Stoneygate's houses.

6 St Martins. Married home of **Agnes Archer Evans**, Leicester headmistress and leader of the Leicester Suffrage Society from 1887.

100 Regent's Road. Final Leicester home of **John Flower**, 'The Leicester Artist'. Born in 1793, Flower studied art in London before returning to his home town. He taught art in Leicester and is famous for his many scenes of life in Leicester and Leicestershire.

Authors

Leicester has produced many well-known authors and playwrights. **Joe Orton**, **Colin Wilson** and **Julian Barnes**, author of *Flaubert's Parrot, A History of the World in 10½ Chapters* and *England, England*, were all born and raised in Leicester.

Few of these authors have stayed in the city. One exception is **Sue Townsend**, the prolific humorous novelist and playwright, best known for her Adrian Mole books. Ms Townsend has drawn upon Leicester to inspire her work, even basing some of Adrian Mole's teachers upon those of her own children. In February 2009 she was given the freedom of the city.

Sue Townsend was the role model for another Leicester author. **Bali Rai** returned to Leicester after graduating from university and published his first novel, *(Un)arranged Marriage*, in 2001 after he was taken on by local agent Jennifer Luithlen. Mr Rai primarily writes for children and young adults.

Musical Leicester

Leicester is the hometown of **Englebert Humperdinck**, R&B's **Mark Morrison** and **Shawaddywaddy**. It was also the birthplace in 1888 of **Lawrence Wright**, composer, music publisher and founder of *Melody Maker* magazine. In 1962, Wright was awarded the Ivor Novello Award for 'outstanding service to British popular and light music'.

Leicester was also the adopted home of **Laurel Aitken**, the grandfather of ska from 1971 until his death in 2005. Aitken is known to have been a major influence on bands such as Madness, the Specials and Bad Manners.

The city's biggest recent successes have been with indie bands. **Cornershop**, who had a hit in 1997 with *Brimful of Asha*, were formed in Leicester in 1991 and played their first gig in the city.

But Leicester's biggest current musical success is **Kasabian**, one of the most successful indie bands in the country. The band, who all originate from local Leicester villages, began recording in Leicester's Bedrock Studios. They still retain close links with the city, with lead singer Tom Meighan a regular shopper at Leicester Market. The band also play special hometown gigs for fans, the last in October 2011 at the O2 academy at Leicester University.

Leicester in Days Gone By:
London Road

Political Figures

In the 1840s Leicester was a stronghold for Chartism –
the first large-scale working-class organisation for political
reform in the world. One of its leaders was **Thomas Cooper**,
a self-educated shoemaker who became a journalist
and author. Born in Leicester in 1805, Cooper worked at
The Leicestershire Mercury before transferring to the chartist
journal *The Commonwealthman*. His militant activities earned
him a two-year jail sentence for sedition and conspiracy,
during which he wrote the poem *Purgatory of the Suicides*.

Just over sixty years later, Britain had its first labour
government led by **Ramsey McDonald.** The future prime
minister began his career in Leicester, when he became one
of its MPs in June 1906.

The first Asian Member of Parliament since Shanurii
Saklatvala in the 1920s, **Keith Vaz** was first elected
for Leicester East in 1987. He is still working for his
community today, making him the longest-standing
Asian MP.

TV Personalities

Leicester has produced a number of actors and TV personalities familiar to viewers. They include:

Gok Wan – Fashion guru and presenter

Terri Dwyer – Actress and presenter, famous for her role as Ruth in *Hollyoaks*

Bill Maynard – Claude Greengrass in *Heartbeat*

Parminder Nagra – Star of *Bend it Like Beckham* and *ER*

Richard Armitage – One of the stars of the BBC's *Robin Hood* and *Spooks*

Maureen 'Biddy' Baxter – Designer of the Blue Peter badge

David Icke – Footballer turned sports presenter who later became infamous for his outlandish conspiracy theories

Graham Chapman – The Cambridge-educated Python was born in 1941 in Stoneygate nursing home

Leicester Bollywood

Leicester is fast becoming a favourite location for Bollywood films, largely because of its Asian population. *Pyaar Ko Kya Naam Doon?* (What Shall I Name This Love?) was the first Bollywood film to be shot entirely in Leicester. Most of the sixty extras and performers were locals. In 2004, *Raakh* (Ashes), a gangster movie, had 50% of its scenes shot around the city.

Bollywood's interest has proven contagious. In 2007, venues such as the University of Leicester's botanical gardens and the Grand Union Canal became part of a TV series called *Samunder Paar*, or 'Overseas'. Telling the story of British Asians, it was screened in India and Britain.

Leicester's Asian film career continues to go from strength to strength. In 2012, the Golden Mile became the city's latest star when it was used as a location for the comedy *Jadoo*. Written and directed by Leicester-born Amit Gupta, the film tells the story of two brothers who run rival Belgrave restaurants, fighting over their mother's recipe books. This time, the cast is more familiar to the general British audience, including Harish Patel, of *Run Fatboy Run*, and Madhur Jaffrey.

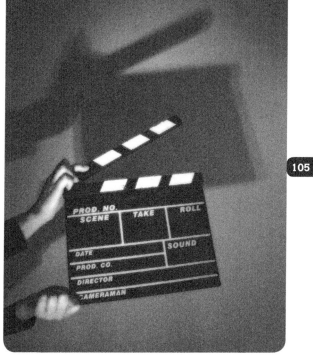

Leicester and Royalty

For a small provincial town, Leicester has had its fair share of dealings with royalty. The town became part of the royal estate when **John of Gaunt's** son became **Henry IV**. **Henry VI** was knighted in the Church of St Mary de Castro and **Richard III** was a frequent visitor to the town before his last fateful stay. The town also played host to **Mary, Queen of Scots**, her son **James I** and **Charles I,** who all stayed in the now demolished Huntingdon Tower which once stood on the High Street.

Royalty has continued to pass through Leicester, even if it hasn't stayed the night. **Queen Victoria and Prince Albert** visited in 1843 and the future **Edward VII** often passed through on his way to Bradgate House when he was Prince of Wales. On one occasion he was invited to return to open Abbey Park. On 10 June 1919, Edward's son **George V** visited Leicester to thank the town for its contribution to the war effort. Four days later, the king restored Leicester to city status.

The most recent royal visit was in March 2012 when **Elizabeth II**'s Diamond Jubilee tour began in the city. The queen, Prince Philip and the Duchess of Cambridge arrived at Leicester station before being treated to a showcase of Leicester talent, Asian dance and music and lunch at the cathedral. Leicester was chosen to kick-start the celebrations because it was felt its cultural diversity best personified modern Britain.

Sporting Heroes

England striker and sports presenter **Gary Lineker** was born and raised in Leicester. Beginning his career with Leicester City, by the age of twenty-four he was on the England squad. He was the team's top scorer in the 1986 World Cup and Footballer of the Year in 1992. He is England's all time second highest scorer behind Bobby Charlton. And all this without ever receiving a red or yellow card.

Another locally born England player who began with Leicester City is **Emile Heskey**. He made a £1 million transfer to Liverpool in 2000 – a record amount at the time.

Known as 'The Binman' because of his day job in Leicester, **Rendall Munroe** rose to fame when he defied the odds and defeated Kiko Martinez to become the 2009 EBU Super Bantam Weight Champion. He was also the 2009 Commonwealth title holder. His trademark is the florescent yellow binman's jacket worn by himself and his corner men.

Football isn't the only ballgame Leicester excels in. **Willie Thorne**, snooker player and commentator, was born in the city. The Willie Thorne Snooker Centre on Charles Street is named in his honour. Still living in Leicester is fellow snooker player **Mark Selby**, runner-up in the World Snooker Championship 2007, and winner of the Masters in 2008.

Leicester Tigers

Leicester's biggest sporting success is Leicester Tigers. The most successful English rugby club since the introduction of Rugby League, 'The Tigers' were founded in 1880. They acquired their distinctive nickname in 1885, either from the club's original brown and yellow kit or from a local regiment who had served time in India, also known as the Tigers.

The team switched to the scarlet, green and white strip in 1895 and moved to their Welford Road home in 1892 where they have gone from strength to strength.

Milestones:

1897 – First won the Midlands County Cup. Repeated the success ever year until 1905. The Tigers then dropped out to 'give other teams a chance'.

1968 – Chalkie White becomes coach. Team successes and supporter numbers increase.

1997 – Six Leicester players named to play in the British Lion's tour of South Africa.

1998-2002 – The Tigers took the premiership title for four years in a row. Became the first team to win the European Cup in successive seasons.

2000/2001 – Won the Heineken Cup.

2000/2001, 2001/2002 – European Champions.

2000/2001, 2001/2002, 2006/2007, 2008/2009, 2009-2010 – English Champions.

2009/10 – Top of the premiership.

Other Sports

Leicester City Football Club was founded in 1884.
It changed its name from Leicester Fosse to commemorate
the restoration of Leicester's city status. Besides Gary
Lineker, famous players at Leicester City have included
Robbie Savage and Steve Walsh.

Grace Road in Aylestone is home to **Leicester County
Cricket Club**, winners of the Twenty20 Cup in 2004, 2006
and 2011.

The Leicester Marathon first began in the 1960s. The event
ceased in the '80s due to dwindling interest but was
revived in the 1990s. Today it is a popular annual event,
with thousands of runners gathering at Victoria Park before
taking to the streets and byways of Leicester.

Extreme Ironing

Leicester is also the birthplace of a modern sporting phenomenon: **extreme ironing**. Founded in 1997, the event combines extreme sporting activities such as rock climbing, skiing, marathon running and even sky and scuba diving with an iron and ironing board.

The sport was invented by Leicester resident Phil Shaw, who, on returning from a hard day at work decided to combine a domestic necessity with his passion for rock climbing. Calling himself 'Steam', he began an international tour in 1999 to promote his new sport. As a result, extreme ironing is now especially popular in Germany, the USA, New Zealand, Australia, South Africa and Fiji. In 2002, the British team won gold and bronze at the first Extreme Ironing World Championships.

Particular Pubs

Leicester's has plenty of pubs with character and originality.
Here's a brief selection:

The Polar Bear
Built around 1700, this is one of Leicester's oldest
pubs. The name is more recent, awarded as a tribute to
Peppy the famous Fox's polar bear whose mints were
manufactured nearby.

The Globe
Dating to 1720, the Globe was once used for Leicester's
hiring fair. Recently, it has been taken back to the nineteenth
century with the reintroduction of gas light, one of only four
pubs in the UK to do so.

The Dry Dock
Partly constructed from an old boat and entered via a gang
plank, this is arguably Leicester's most novel pub. It was
built in 1997.

The Donkey
With the closure of the much-loved Charlotte in 2010, this
former watering hole for travellers pausing at the Welford
Road tollgate is now Leicester's best-loved live music venue,
playing host to acts like Michelle Shocked, the Fun Lovin'
Criminals, Miles Hunt and the Drugstore Cowboys.

The Old Horse
Another old tollgate pub built in 1850, the Old Horse once
served thirsty travellers and the patrons of the Victoria Park
racecourse. Today it provides food and beer for revellers at
the many events the park hosts, as well as families taking
advantage of its beer garden.

The Pub
Situated along New Walk, the Pub has the largest selection of
draught beers in Leicester, including UK ales and foreign beers.

Leicester in Days Gone By:
The Station

Not a Lot of People Know That...

In 1963, Leicester was the first city in Europe to have an automatic multi-storey car park.

In the same year, it was the first UK city outside London to have a Tesco supermarket.

Leicester almost became a spa town in the late eighteenth and early nineteenth centuries. Two springs were discovered, but despite being equipped with fine spa buildings the venture never took off. One of the springs gave its name to an area of the city: Newfoundpool.

Established in 1960, the Taj Mahal, Highfields, is the oldest Indian restaurant in Leicester.

In 1967, Radio Leicester was the UK's first local radio station to broadcast.

Grooves in the stonework of The Magazine were supposedly made by pikemen sharpening their weapons.

The phrase 'Mi duck' isn't as casual as it sounds. It derives from the Anglo-Saxon 'duka' or duke.

New Walk follows part of the route of the Via Devana Roman road.

The long window in the left-hand turret of Leicester Prison used to be the door to the condemned cell.

Leicester Abbey was the second richest in England before its dissolution.

Humberstone Gate was made wider than the surrounding streets to accommodate the annual Leicester Fair.

Modern Hamilton is named after a nearby deserted medieval village.

The design of the glass frontage of Leicester's John Lewis is in fact a motif from the store's archives.

Future Plans

A £4 million square is proposed for St Nicholas Place to commemorate the queen's Jubilee visit. Complete with gardens and cafés, the centrepiece of the square will be the remains of the sixteenth-century high cross monument. This will be moved from its current position near Leicester Market so that it is closer to its original site on Highcross Street.

The out-of-place 1960s city council buildings at the bottom of New Walk are to be demolished. There is a proposal to build new environmentally friendly headquarters on the same spot, more in proportion with the nearby buildings.

A new airport lounge-style bus station is to be built in 2014 to replace the current St Margaret's bus station. It is part of a city-wide scheme to improve public transport and encourage people to use it in the city centre.

Before You Go...

Go on a ghost walk

Watch Leicester Tigers play at home

Learn how to mix cocktails at Hotel Maiyango, caterers for the queen's visit

Visit the National Space Centre

Take a bus tour of the city

Visit the Golden Mile for truly authentic curry

Enjoy a pint of Everards' finest by gaslight in The Globe

Shop along The Lanes, Allendale and Queen's Roads

Relax with an ice cream on the banks of the River Soar in Abbey Park

Take a trip into the Leicestershire countryside via steam train from the Great Central Railway's Leicester North Station.

Picture Credits

Unless otherwise credited, all pictures were taken by the author.

3. Leicester's coat of arms – De Monfort Hall (Credit: Neil Bate)
7. Leicester city skyline (Credit: Mat Fascione)
9. The Guildhall; The Shakespeare Pub, Southgates
11. Leicester Clock Tower
13. Churchgate – with St Margaret's Church at the end
15. The Great Hall of Leicester Castle, as viewed from Castle Gardens; The Church of St Mary Magdalene, at the centre of the old village of Knighton
17. Queenstown, New Zealand (Credit: Donald Y. Tong)
19. The National Space Centre (Credit: Ned Trifle); Leicester Cathedral; The former County Asylum buildings, now the administrative offices of the University of Leicester (Credit: Neil Bate)
21. Haskovo Square (Credit: Nenko Lazaror)
23. Town Hall, Leicester, Massachusetts (Credit: Pumoutside); Leicester Town Hall, UK
24. Wall of the Roman Baths, Jewry Wall, with the ancient church of St Nicholas in the background
25. Leicester railway station; De Monfort University
27. The Curve Theatre in the cultural quarter; The Polar Bear pub, Oxford Street
31. The Jain Temple, Oxford Street; The Highcross Shopping Centre
33. Granby Street c. 1906
35. Leicester Market with the Corn Exchange in the background; Former offices of Thomas Cook on Gallowtree Gate
37. Santander Building – the replacement for Leicester's Theatre Royal; To let signs on Granby Street
39. Writing (SXC)
41. St George's Tower
43. Top Hat Towers, London Road; Welford Road Prison
45. Gallowtree Gate postcard
47. The Abbey Pumping Station (Credit: Richard Rogerson)
49. New Walk Museum and Art Gallery
51. Victoria Park, with the University of Leicester's Attenborough Building in the background; Watermead County Park (Credit: Mat Fascione)

53. The Eco House (with the permission of Neil Hart); Bike Park sign from Leicester Town Hall
55. McIndians
57. Everard's Brewery at Fosse Park, Leicester (Credit: Mat Fascione)
59. Astronomical Clock, the University of Leicester (Credit: Alun Salt)
61. Cardinal Wolsey. Photograph of picture by Sampson Strong, *c.* 1526
63. Greyfriars excavation, 2012 – burial site of Richard III (Credit: University of Leicester)
65. John Merrick, *c.* 1889. (Photographer unknown – Royal London Hospital Archives)
67. Statue of Simon De Monfort on Clock Tower, Leicester city centre
69. Corn exchange postcard
71. The Leader of the Luddites, *c.* 1812. Author unknown
73. The Occupy Leicester Camp, December 2011 (Picture courtesy of Occupy Leicester)
73. Bowstring Bridge before its demolition (Credit: NotfromUtrecht)
75. Ronald Light after his acquittal. Contemporary press photograph, 1920
77. Witch (SXC, Credit: ciscopa)
79. Statue of Richard III, Castle Gardens
81. St Nicholas Church postcard.
83. Leicester Cathedral churchyard; The Marquis of Wellington pub, London Road
85. South gate of Leicester Castle – the haunt of Black Annis
87. The Magazine Gateway, the last remains of the defences of Leicester; Leicester war memorial, Victoria Park
89. Mouth (SXC)
91. Diwali festivities along Belgrave Road (Credit: Kiran Parmar); Leicester Caribbean Carnival (Credit: Andy T.)
93. Thorncroft House, London Road; College House, University of Leicester; 118 New Walk – now part of the Belmont Hotel
95. Joe Orton's commemorative plaque near Orton Square in the cultural quarter
97. Kasabian (Credit: Chris Worden)
99. London Road postcard.
101. Ramsey McDonald (Library of Congress)
103. Parminder Nagra (Credit: Gage Skidmore)

105. Film Clapper (SXC)
107. The queen, Duchess of Cambridge and Leicester mayor, Peter Soulsby, during the queen's Diamond Jubilee visit to Leicester, March 2012 (Credit: Peter Warzymski)
109. Gary Lineker carrying the Olympic torch through Leicester (Peter Warzymski)
111. Tiger's Stadium, Welford Road
113. Leicester Marathon competitors running along the Great Central Way (Credit: Stephen McKay)
115. Sky ironing (courtesy of www.extremeironing.com)
117. The Dry Dock pub, Freeman's Common; The Globe, Silver Street
119. Midland Stations, as it was then, in around 1906.
121. New Walk; Humberstone Gate, Leicester city centre
123. The old Highcross, currently located in Leicester Market; The soon to be demolished council buildings at the end of New Walk
125. Loseby Lane, part of 'The Lanes', Leicester city centre; Leicester North Station, the Great Central Railway (Credit: Pete Hackney)

Visit our website and discover thousands of other History Press books.

www.thehistorypress.co.uk

Printed in Great Britain
by Amazon